Friendship

BY TAMARA NEAL

illustrations by Lauren Lacy

Friendship

BY TAMARA NEAL

illustrations by Lauren Lacy

ISBN-13: 978-1500156183 (Create Space-Assigned)
ISBN-10: 1500156183
BISAC: Juvenile Nonfiction / General

This book is dedicated, in loving memory,
to my mom, Brenda Taylor.
She was a compassionate paraprofessional who
worked for the board of education
with special needs children.
She was fondly known as
Mrs. Brenda.

Hi! My name is Christopher,
and I am a friend to all of mankind.
Let's take a look at some of the different
types of friendships that you may easily find!

The Universe is populated with many
different types of friends.
Some friends are real; some are
make pretend.
Some friends have red hair; some
have black.
Some friends have bald heads covered
with hats.
Some friends tweet; some friends quack!
Some friends sleep on beds; some
sleep on mats.
I like all friends.
Now, what do you think about that?

Some friends are skinny; some are fat.
Some friends like puppies; some like cats.
Some friends don't walk; some can't talk.
Some friends say meow; some just bark!

Some friends like to play jump rope.
Some friends like to look through microscopes!
It really doesn't matter how my friends
may look or play.
My friends are all friendly, in their
own special way!

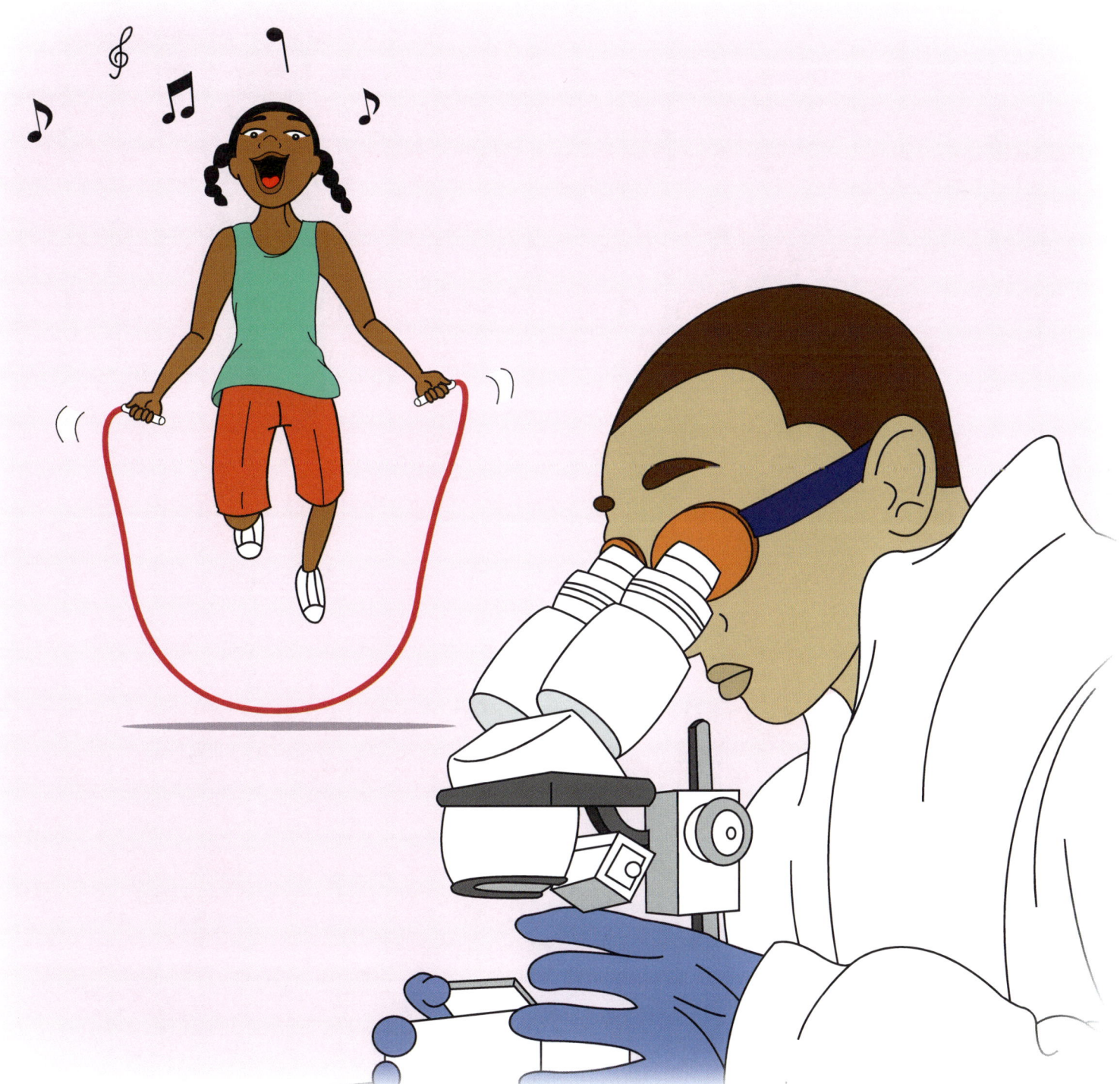

Some of my friends speak
English, Spanish, French, Russian, Portuguese,
or even Chinese.
Some speak German or Swahili with ease.
There are many other languages that my
friends speak. I just named a few.
Do you have friends that
speak different languages, too?

Some friends live in apartments,
surrounded by playgrounds,
other children, and park benches.

Some friends live in houses surrounded by flowers and pretty white fences!

Some friends can't walk,
so they ride on chairs that have wheels.
How my friends move around
is really no big deal!

Some friends like to yell
and scream really loud.
Others talk with their hands
and are just as proud!

Some friends are in the hospital
because they are really sick.
Some friends can't see,
so they carry long sticks.

Some friends have sisters.
Some friends have brothers.
Some friends have more than one father,
and some friends have
two mothers!

Friends are never bullies,
and bullying in friendship is not allowed.
Friendships should always
be friendly and should always
make you proud!

It takes all types of friendships to
make the world go around.
Friends are really special people,
that are very easily found!

The End

Made in the USA
Charleston, SC
29 June 2014